WHAT
makes
us
human

Victor D. O. Santos

WHAT makes us human

illustrations by
Anna Forlati

Eerdmans Books for Young Readers
Grand Rapids, Michigan

I have been around for a very long time.

Longer than toys, dogs, or anyone you know.

My roots go back many centuries.

Some of them even longer.

I am everywhere. In every country, every city,
every school, and every house.

I am sure you saw me today.

Or heard me. Or felt me.

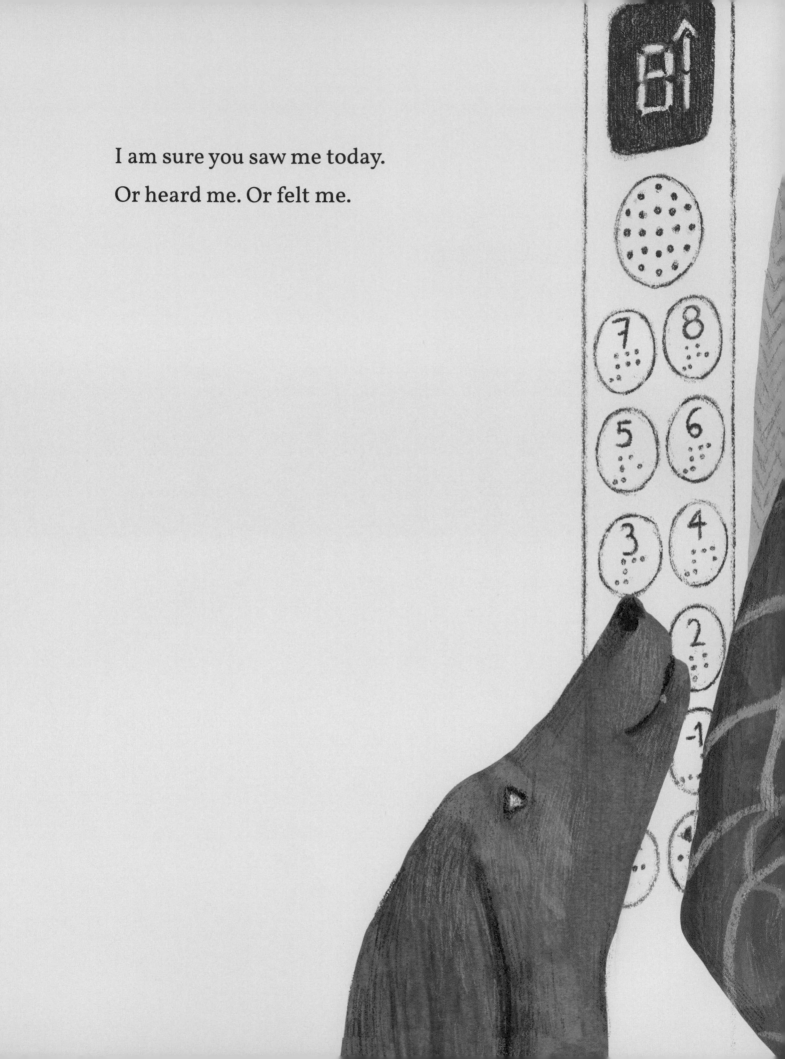

When you were a baby, you hardly knew me.

Over time, you have gotten to know me better and better.

But when you are old, you may start to forget me.

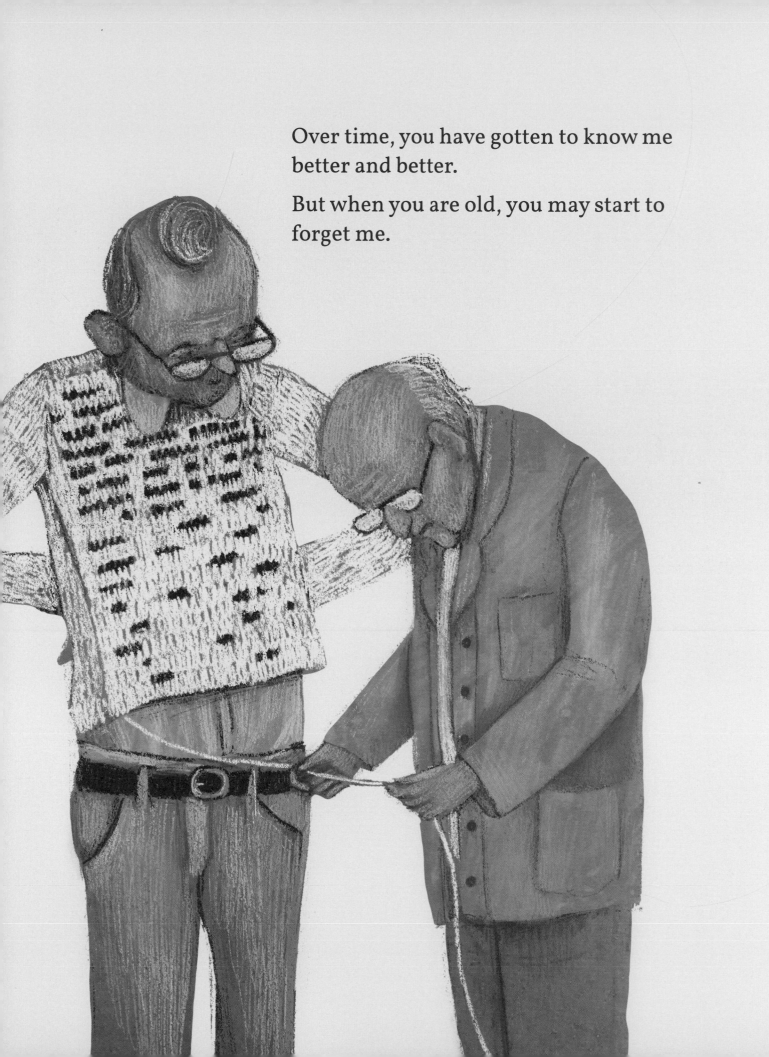

Some people have tried to avoid me.

But they cannot get me out of their heads.

I can be as soft as a kitten or as harsh
as the Alaskan winter.

I can show you love. But also hurt you.

In the beginning, I was one.

But now, you can find me in many
different shapes and forms.

There are thousands of me in the world.
Some are young and some very old.

Some are disappearing quickly.

By the time you grow up, too many could be gone.

And when one of me disappears, a culture may also disappear. A unique way to view and understand the world.

Gone. Forever.

Some people only have one of me. Others, two. Others, more.

More of me means a more colorful and diverse world.

A world with more doors you can open. And more people you can ask to help open those doors.

I am the greatest invention of all. Without me, most others would not exist, including the children's books you love so much.

I can connect you to the past,
the present, and the future.

I make you human.

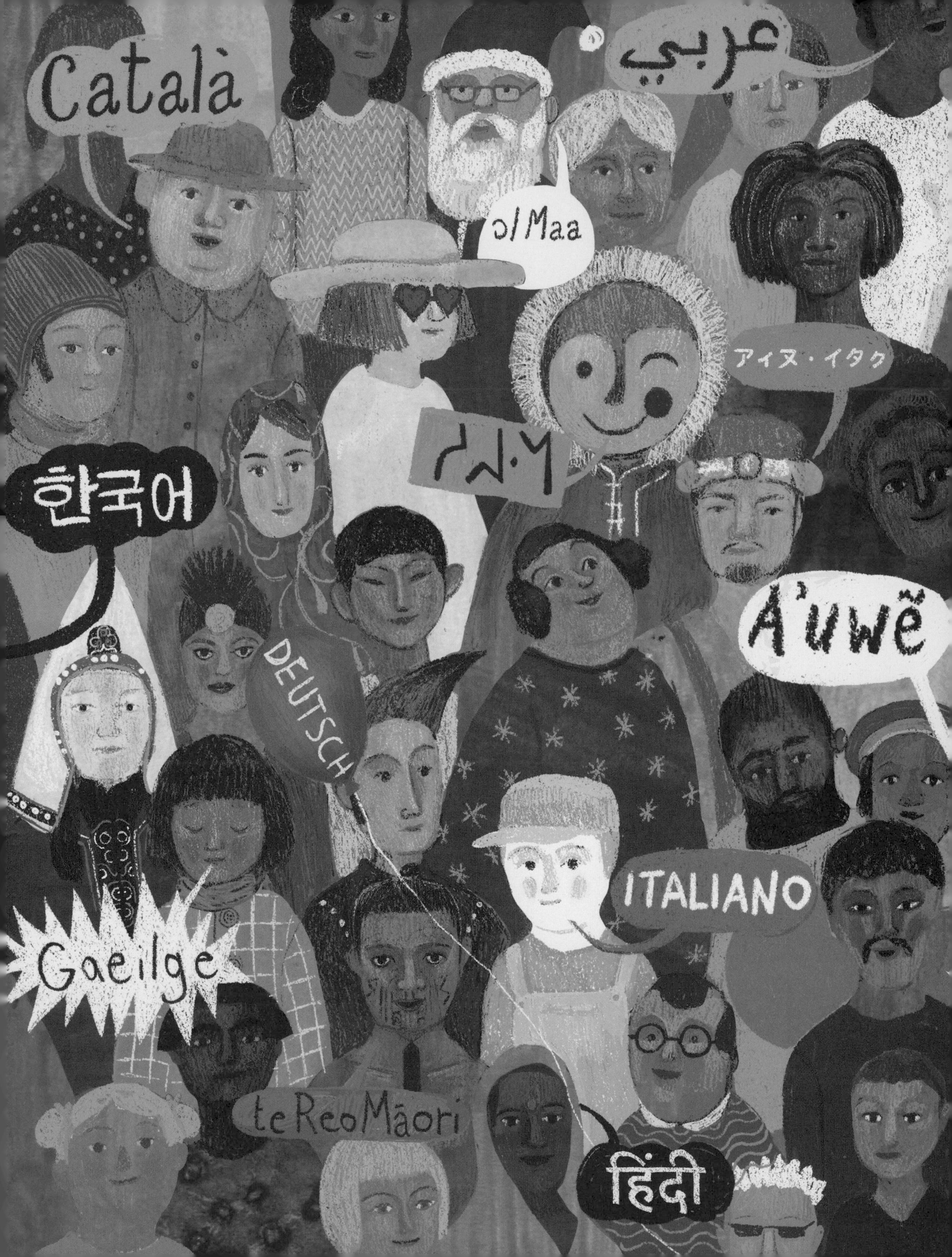

ᏣᎳᎩ ᎦᏬᏂᎯᏍᏗ
Magyar
Português
አማርኛ
עברית
ESPAÑOL
ᐊᓂᔑᓈᐯᒧᐎᓐ
I AM LANGUAGE.
Esperanto
ภาษาไทย
Українська
Diné Bizaad
中文
Ελληνικά
EUSKARA

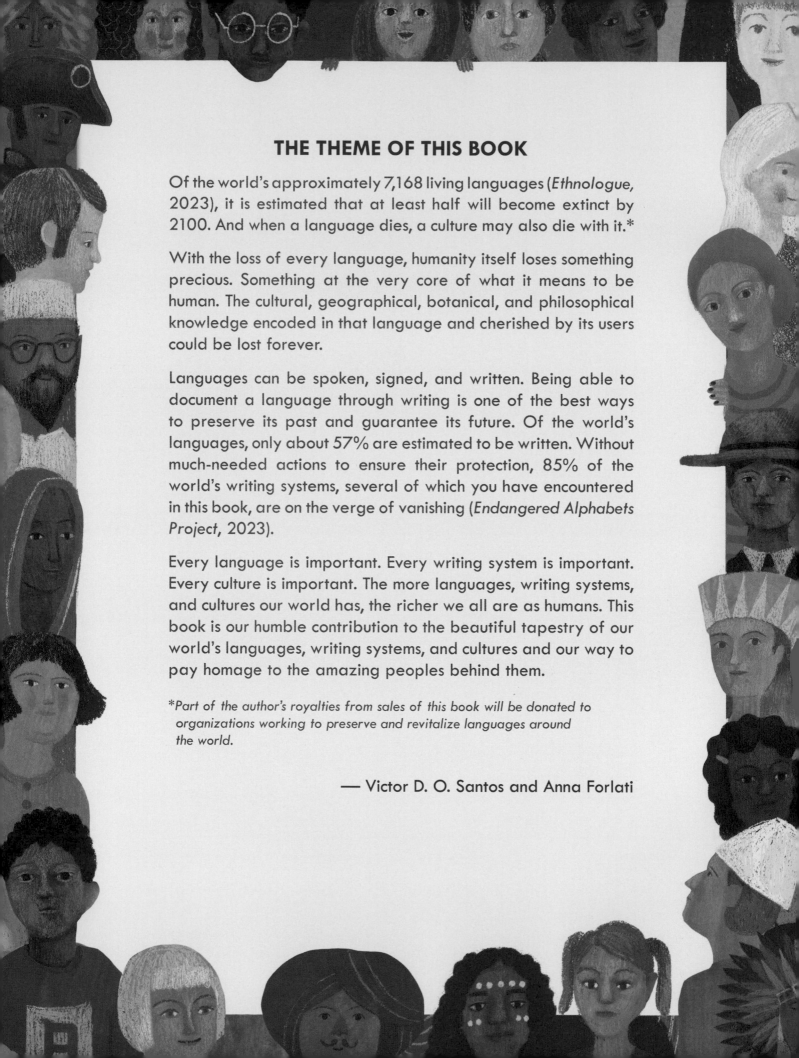

THE THEME OF THIS BOOK

Of the world's approximately 7,168 living languages (*Ethnologue,* 2023), it is estimated that at least half will become extinct by 2100. And when a language dies, a culture may also die with it.*

With the loss of every language, humanity itself loses something precious. Something at the very core of what it means to be human. The cultural, geographical, botanical, and philosophical knowledge encoded in that language and cherished by its users could be lost forever.

Languages can be spoken, signed, and written. Being able to document a language through writing is one of the best ways to preserve its past and guarantee its future. Of the world's languages, only about 57% are estimated to be written. Without much-needed actions to ensure their protection, 85% of the world's writing systems, several of which you have encountered in this book, are on the verge of vanishing (*Endangered Alphabets Project,* 2023).

Every language is important. Every writing system is important. Every culture is important. The more languages, writing systems, and cultures our world has, the richer we all are as humans. This book is our humble contribution to the beautiful tapestry of our world's languages, writing systems, and cultures and our way to pay homage to the amazing peoples behind them.

*Part of the author's royalties from sales of this book will be donated to organizations working to preserve and revitalize languages around the world.

— Victor D. O. Santos and Anna Forlati

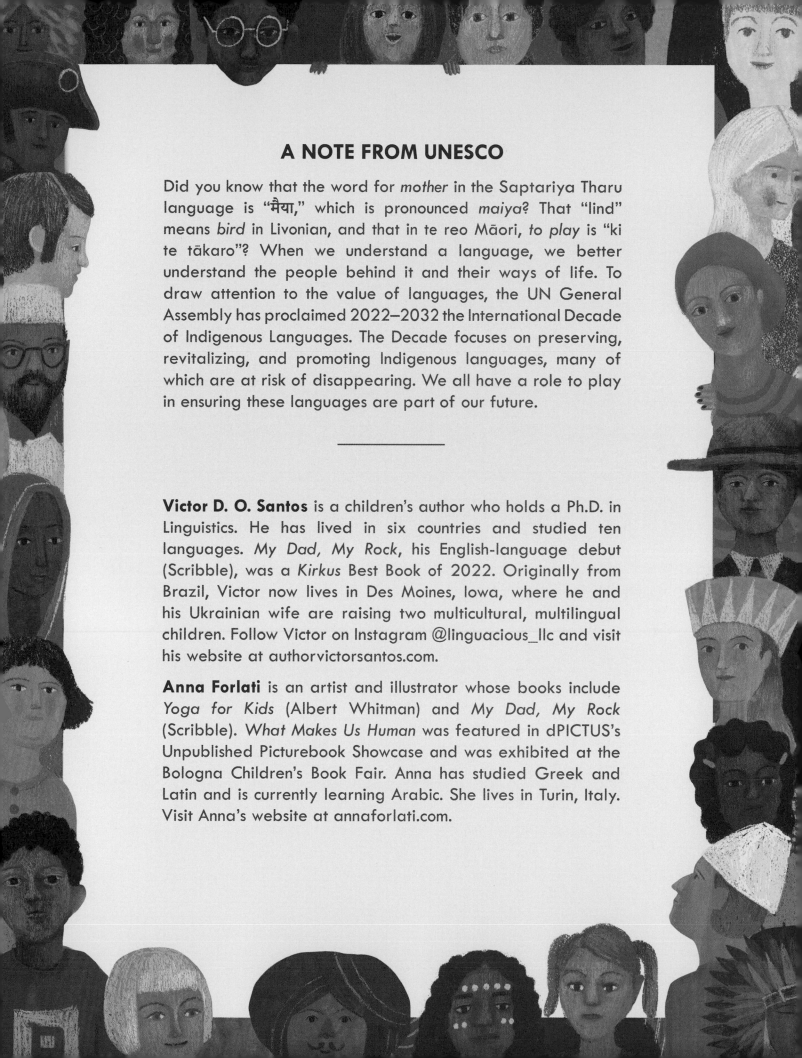

A NOTE FROM UNESCO

Did you know that the word for *mother* in the Saptariya Tharu language is "मैया," which is pronounced *maiya*? That "lind" means *bird* in Livonian, and that in te reo Māori, *to play* is "ki te tākaro"? When we understand a language, we better understand the people behind it and their ways of life. To draw attention to the value of languages, the UN General Assembly has proclaimed 2022–2032 the International Decade of Indigenous Languages. The Decade focuses on preserving, revitalizing, and promoting Indigenous languages, many of which are at risk of disappearing. We all have a role to play in ensuring these languages are part of our future.

———————

Victor D. O. Santos is a children's author who holds a Ph.D. in Linguistics. He has lived in six countries and studied ten languages. *My Dad, My Rock*, his English-language debut (Scribble), was a *Kirkus* Best Book of 2022. Originally from Brazil, Victor now lives in Des Moines, Iowa, where he and his Ukrainian wife are raising two multicultural, multilingual children. Follow Victor on Instagram @linguacious_llc and visit his website at authorvictorsantos.com.

Anna Forlati is an artist and illustrator whose books include *Yoga for Kids* (Albert Whitman) and *My Dad, My Rock* (Scribble). *What Makes Us Human* was featured in dPICTUS's Unpublished Picturebook Showcase and was exhibited at the Bologna Children's Book Fair. Anna has studied Greek and Latin and is currently learning Arabic. She lives in Turin, Italy. Visit Anna's website at annaforlati.com.